Born to be Wild
Little Bees

Valérie Guidoux

Words that appear in the glossary are printed in
boldface type the first time they occur in the text.

GARETH**STEVENS**
GS
P U B L I S H I N G
A WRC Media Company

The Queen Bee

In the bottom of a beehive, the queen bee lays an egg in every **honeycomb** cell, or **alveolus**. Soon, a wormlike **larva** comes out of each egg. These tiny worms think about nothing but eating. Worker bees take turns bringing them food, and the larvae grow quickly. After a week, the bees lock one larva in each of the honeycomb's cells, closing the openings with small pieces of wax.

A queen bee spends her entire life laying eggs. She is the mother of the entire **colony**. When a queen bee lays eggs, a few worker bees surround her, helping and feeding her. They are the queen's daughters, born just a few weeks earlier.

What do you think?

What do bee larvae do in their honeycomb cells?

a) They become grown-up honeybees.

b) They eat their food supplies.

c) They sleep, waiting to be let out of the cells.

In their honeycomb cells, bee larvae become grown-up honeybees.

Like most other **insects**, a honeybee goes through a **metamorphosis**. It spends the first part of its life as a larva. Then, during a period of rest, it changes completely into an adult. After twelve days in a honeycomb cell, a young honeybee comes out perfectly formed.

From the time it first sticks its head out of its cell, a worker bee will live only five to six weeks — but it will not waste a minute of that time.

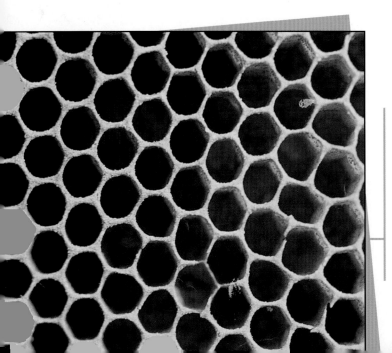

Honeycombs are divided into six-sided cells, called alveoli. Some cells are used to store **nectar**, honey, or **pollen**, while other cells contain eggs or larvae. The biggest cells hold the larvae of male bees. These bees are called drones.

Worker bees are female bees that cannot **reproduce**. They do all
the work in the colony, including feeding the larvae. The larvae of
worker bees are first fed royal jelly, a creamy and healthy substance
that comes from the heads of young worker bees. The larvae are
then fed bee bread, which is a mixture of pollen and honey.

Busy As a Bee

As soon as a young worker bee comes out of its cell, it stretches and unfolds its legs and wings. The little bee immediately starts to eat and grow stronger. Then it gets to work. Like all other honeybees, it knows what it has to do. A worker bee's job starts with three days of cleaning the hive. Even if the hive is very clean, there is always a dead bee to throw away, a few scraps to clear out, and some cells to clean.

A worker bee's first job in the hive is as a nurse. A nurse bee feeds the larvae and the younger bees by passing food from her mouth to theirs. Honeybees often share food with each other this way.

What do you think?

The inside of a beehive is very dark. How do honeybees avoid bumping into each other?

a) Their yellow stripes glow in the dark.

b) They can see in the dark, like cats.

c) They feel and smell each other with their **antennae.**

6

In the darkness of their hives, honeybees feel and smell each other with their antennae.

A honeybee's senses of smell and touch are extremely sensitive. Tiny sense organs on a honeybee's antennae make it able to smell the faint scents given off by other bees. Little hairs on their antennae probably help the bees feel.

Inside the hive, each of the tens of thousands of worker bees always knows exactly what to do. Although they don't have a leader, the bees use their senses to constantly communicate with each other.

Honeybees wash themselves often. Their antennae and legs must be kept clean so the bees can use them to communicate. Bees exchange information by touching and smelling.

A worker bee becomes a nurse when it is four days old. For only a few days, its body will produce the precious royal jelly that it uses to feed the larvae. A nurse bee also feeds some of its jelly to the queen bee.

When it is twelve days old, a worker bee changes jobs because its body starts making wax. All the wax makers work together in a line, passing along small pieces of wax to create the **symmetrical** cells that make up the honeycomb.

When a worker bee is eighteen days old, its body stops making wax, and its job building the hive is over. The worker's next job is guarding the hive's entrance. As soon as a strange bee enters the hive, it is stung, killed, and thrown out of the hive.

Hurray for Flowers!

At three weeks of age, a worker bee is ready to begin its final task — making honey. At last, the honeybee leaves the hive and discovers the outside world. When a bee leaves the honeycomb, it has a serious job to do. Flying from flower to flower, there is no time for fun. The bee must collect either nectar or pollen. While the bee works, it has to be careful to avoid spider webs, insect-eating birds, and many other dangers.

A bee collecting nectar or pollen travels as far as 2 miles (3 kilometers) away from its hive. From sunrise to sunset, the bee makes many trips. Sometimes, it carries nectar, other times pollen.

What do you think?

Why are honeybees useful to flowers?

a) because they chase butterflies away

b) because they carry pollen

c) because they eat ladybugs

Honeybees carry pollen, which flowers need to reproduce.

As honeybees fly around gathering nectar and pollen, they help flowers at the same time! When a bee lands on a flower, some of the flower's pollen gets trapped in the bee's hair. When the bee flies to other flowers, it drops pollen onto them. Carrying pollen from plant to plant helps flowers reproduce.

A honeybee must visit hundreds of flowers to gather enough nectar to fill the pouch, or crop, inside its stomach. Using its long, tubelike tongue, the bee sucks the nectar out of flowers.

As a worker bee gathers pollen, it shapes the grains into a tiny ball. The bee carries pollen back to the hive in a basket on its back legs.

In the hive, bees unload the pollen they have gathered. Bees bringing nectar to the hive pass the nectar from mouth to mouth to other bees.

When a bee finds a field of flowers, it flies to the hive to tell the other bees. It communicates by performing a dance in a figure-eight pattern, which points the bees to the field of flowers.

A Honey Factory

Honeybees that collect nectar never stop working, especially if they live in a beekeeper's hive. A beekeeper is a person who raises honeybees. To increase honey production, a beekeeper adds many layers of honeycomb to the nesting boxes, or hives. Hardworking honeybees will produce as much honey as they need to fill up the combs. Bees that live in a beekeeper's hive are able to produce a lot more honey than bees living in wild nests found in trees, caves, or other hollow places.

What do you think?

What is the humming sound that a bee makes?

a) the movement of its wings

b) the noise it makes to scare away its enemies

c) its voice when it talks to other bees

The taste of honey depends on the type of flower from which honeybees take the nectar. This field of lavender will help the bees in nearby hives produce one flavor of honey. Nectar from orange blossoms, clover, or rosemary will produce different flavors. Because of the tie between flowers and flavors, various types of honey depend on the locations of the beehives.

A bee's humming sound is the movement of its wings.

Even though honeybees don't fly inside the hive, their humming is still very loud. Worker bees fan their wings in front of the combs to evaporate the water in the honey, which makes the honey thicker. During summer, these little fans help keep the inside of the hive at a constant temperature of 95° Fahrenheit (35° Celius).

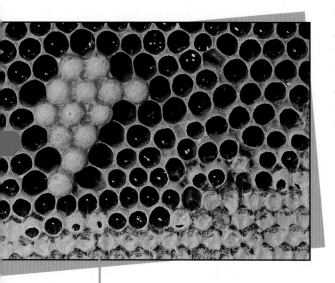

Honey is a kind of syrup made from nectar. Bees thicken honey by fanning fresh air through it and kneading, or pushing, on it. When the honey is ready, the bees store it in honeycomb cells, which they seal with wax.

People are not the only ones who like honey! Bears are willing to face the stings of many bees to eat honey from a wild hive.

To collect honey, a beekeeper lifts off a hive's roof and removes the honeycombs the bees have filled.

Honeybees stay in their hives during winter. For food, they eat honey. The queen bee starts laying eggs when warm weather returns and the workers are ready to feed the larvae.

Life in a Hive

At the height of summer, up to fifty thousand bees can be busy inside and around a hive. Some worker bees clean, others feed the drones, or male bees, who cannot eat by themselves. Still other workers build new cells, guard the hive, or collect nectar. The queen bee spends her days laying eggs. She can lay up to three thousand a day, but if she always layed eggs at this rate, the hive would blow up!

Drones are the male bees in the hive. Their only job is to mate with the queen bee. Most drones die by the end of summer without having done anything at all!

What do you think?

What happens in a hive when there are too many bees?

a) The queen stops laying eggs.

b) The queen moves out with some of the workers.

c) The workers kill each other.

19

When there are too many bees in a hive, the queen moves out with some of the workers.

Before a queen moves out of a crowded hive, she lays eggs in special cells for queen bees. Worker bees will feed only royal jelly to the larvae from these eggs, which will give the new female bees the ability to reproduce. Just before the new bees are born, the old queen leaves the hive with a group of bees to look for a new nest. When bees move in a group, it is called **swarming**.

When the queen leaves a hive, she is protected by a swarm, or group, of workers who form a tight ball around her. Some bees fly ahead to find the right place for a new hive. It might be in a cave, a hollow tree, or a beekeeper's hive.

To attract a swarm to a prepared hive, a beekeeper gently catches the swarm and puts it in a box before placing it in an empty hive. While they are swarming, bees are very quiet and do not sting.

Only one queen can rule a colony. If more than one queen is born at the same time, they will fight. The bee who stings and kills its rivals wins.

A queen bee mates only one day. When she is ready to mate she leaves the hive, followed by many drones. Bees mate while they are flying. After the queen has mated, she returns to the hive to lay her eggs. She will not leave the hive again unless she moves to a new hive as part of a swarm.

Honeybees are insects. They live in woods, hedges, and meadows in areas of Europe, Asia, and North America with mild climates. Honeybees range from ½ to 1 inch (1 to 2 centimeters) long, with queen bees being a little larger than worker bees. Worker bees live five to six weeks, while a queen can live three to four years.

Honeybees belong to the bee family, which includes four hundred species of bees and bumblebees.

When a worker bee collects nectar, it stores it in a pouch, called a crop, inside its abdomen.

The stinger is located at the tip of a bee's abdomen.

Each of a honeybee's back legs has a kind of basket where it stores the pollen it takes from flowers.

Bees have a tiny claw on each of their front legs, which they use to clean their antennae.

A honeybee uses its wings to fly and to fan air through the inside of the hive.

Each of a honeybee's eyes has six thousand individual flat surfaces. Its eyes allow a bee to see all around itself, but it cannot see very clearly.

Honeybees use their two very sensitive antennae to smell.

Suction cups and hooks on a honeybee's legs help it hang on to flowers and the honeycomb.

A honeybee has a **proboscis**, which is a tubelike tongue the bee uses to suck up nectar.

23

GLOSSARY

alveolus — a honeycomb cell, multiple cells are called alveoli

antennae — the long, thin body parts on an insect's head

colony — a group of the same kind of animal or plant living or growing together

honeycomb — a structure of many six-sided cells made by honeybees to hold honey, pollen, nectar, eggs, and larvae

insects — animals with six legs, two antenna, a body divided into three main parts, and wings

larva — the wormlike form of a newly hatched insect

metamorphosis — a complete change in form or appearance

nectar — the sweet liquid in flowers that bees gather to make honey

pollen — the powderlike, male cells produced by flowers. Pollen grains fertilize the female parts of flowers.

proboscis — a kind of tube that sticks out of an insect's head and is used for sucking liquids

reproduce — to produce young

swarming — moving in a group, or swarm, from one place to another

symmetrical — having parts that match and that are exactly the same size and shape on all sides of an object

Please visit our web site at: **www.garethstevens.com**
For a free color catalog describing Gareth Stevens Publishing's list of high-quality books and multimedia programs, call 1-800-542-2595 (USA) or 1-800-387-3178 (Canada). Gareth Stevens Publishing's fax: (414) 332-3567.

Library of Congress Cataloging-in-Publication Data

Guidoux, Valérie.
   [L' abeille. English]
   Little bees / Valérie Guidoux. — North American ed.
      p. cm. — (Born to be wild)
     ISBN 0-8368-4433-5 (lib. bdg.)
     I. Title. II. Series.
   QL568.A6G7813 2004
   595.79'9—dc22   2004057437

This North American edition first published in 2005 by
Gareth Stevens Publishing
A WRC Media Company
330 West Olive Street, Suite 100
Milwaukee, Wisconsin 53212 USA

First published in 2001 as *L' abeille* by Mango Jeunesse, an imprint of Editions Mango, Paris, France.

Picture Credits [top = t, bottom = b, left = l, right = r]
Bios: Fr. Gilson 8(tr), 21(tr); D. Bringard 3, 16(r); M. Harvey 20; C. Laurier back cover, 11; G. Meilhac 22(l). Colibri: R. Toulouse 4(b); J. M. Pouyfourcat 9(t); G. Bonnafous 12; Ch. Haug 13(bl); K. Etienne 15; Negro/Cretu 16(l); L. Chaix 17(t). Jacana: F. Winner 4(t); P. Lorne 10; F. Winner 22-23. Phone: Cl. Jardel cover, 2, 9(b), 13(t), 21(tl); P. Olivier 13(br); Ch. Courteau 17(b); P. Goetgheluck title page, 18. Sunset: Animals Animals 5; P. Lorne 7, 19; NHPA 8(bl); P. Moulu 21(b).

English translation: Muriel Castille
Gareth Stevens editor: Barbara Kiely Miller
Gareth Stevens art direction: Tammy West

Printed in the United States of America

1 2 3 4 5 6 7 8 9 09 08 07 06 05